Schools Council
Research Studies

WITHDRAWN

A Science Teaching
Observation Schedule

This first report from the Schools Council Project for the Evaluation of Science Teaching Methods describes the construction and use of an observation instrument devised by the project to record intellectual transactions taking place during science lessons

OTHER BOOKS IN THIS SERIES

The Universities and the Sixth Form Curriculum
Entry and Performance at Oxford and Cambridge, 1966–71
Pattern and Variation in Curriculum Development Projects
The Examination of Courses of First Year Sixth Formers
Mass Media and the Secondary School
Paths to University: Preparation, Assessment, Selection
Gifted Children in Primary Schools
Evaluation in Curriculum Development Projects: Twelve
    Case Studies
Some Aspects of Welsh and English: a Survey in the
    Schools of Wales
Attitudes to Welsh and English in the Schools of Wales
Purpose, Power and Constraint in the Primary School
    Curriculum
A Level Syllabus Studies
Physical Education in Secondary Schools
Pre-school Education
The Quality of Listening
The Effects of Environmental Factors on Secondary
    Educational Attainment in Manchester: a Plowden
    Follow-up
Nuffield Secondary Science: an Evaluation
Environmental Studies Project (5–13): an Evaluation
Education of Travelling Children
Authority and Organization in the Secondary School
The Aims of Primary Education: a Study of Teachers'
    Opinions
Science 5–13: a Formative Evaluation
O Level Examined: the Effect of Question Choice

Schools Council
Research Studies

A Science Teaching Observation Schedule

J. F. Eggleston
M. J. Galton
M. E. Jones

WITHDRAWN

M

Macmillan Education

First published 1975

SBN 333 17613 8

Published by
MACMILLAN EDUCATION LTD
London and Basingstoke

Associated companies and representatives
throughout the world

Printed in Great Britain by
Hazell Watson & Viney Ltd, Aylesbury, Bucks

Foreword

The Schools Council Project for the Evaluation of Science Teaching Methods, based at the University of Leicester School of Education, has used three measuring instruments in the course of its work. Two of these, which measure attitudes and attainment, were modified versions of existing instruments. The third, a Science Teaching Observation Schedule, was constructed by the project team. It is the first work of this particular kind to be produced in the United Kingdom and the Council is now making it available for research workers and science teachers.

It is necessary to stress that this observation schedule is not in itself an evaluation instrument. It is rather a method of recording, with a high degree of accuracy, those intellectual exchanges which take place in classrooms. There is no suggestion that certain types of exchanges are in some arbitrary fashion to be designated 'good' or 'bad', 'desirable' or 'undesirable'. It is only when the results derived from using the schedule are analysed in relation to a great deal of other information that any association between teaching styles and the outcomes of teaching might be discernible. Members of the research team at Leicester are currently undertaking this kind of analysis and have prepared a report on their findings.

The observation schedule has been thoroughly researched in over 100 schools. However, it is important for other users of the schedule to recognize that the results quoted here are derived from a necessarily limited sample of pupils in the above-average (but not in the highest) ability range. This limitation was due to the need to restrict the number of variables in the research, but the schedule can be used with any sample of pupils.

Any research worker who wishes to use the observation schedule will appreciate that a short course of training is necessary. Such a course, using videotape recordings, was provided for the observers who participated in the experimental work and is now available to others as described on p. xii.

Research into what actually happens in classrooms is a difficult undertaking made possible only through the willing and active co-operation of teachers. During the production of this observation schedule the research team were offered such co-operation by large numbers of teachers. In making the schedule available the Schools Council acknowledges with gratitude the contribution of these teachers as well as that of the tutors who acted as observers.

Contents

Foreword   v
Tables and figures   ix
Acknowledgements   x
Materials for the Science Teaching Observation Schedule   xii

1   **The Science Teaching Observation Schedule**   1
Origin of the schedule   1
Development of the schedule   3
The Science Teaching Observation Schedule   5
Suggested procedure for using the schedule   7
Training   10
Reliability   11
Subsequent use of the schedule   16

2   **User's manual**   18
Introduction   18
Sampling and scoring   18
Generalized descriptions of the schedule (ten ground rules)   19
Summary of the rules to be applied when using the schedule   24
Examples of the use of categories   25
Further examples involving more complex interactions   29

3   **Observers' reactions**   33
Some problems associated with particular categories   33
General comments   38

Tables and figures

Table 1 Coefficients of agreement for twenty-one observers using
the schedule   12

    2 Measures of group reliability for twenty-one observers
using the schedule   16

Figure 1 'Black box' model of the comparative approach to curriculum evaluation   2

    2 Main features of the classification used in the Science
Teaching Observation Schedule   6

    3 The Science Teaching Observation Schedule   8

Acknowledgements

The project team would like to thank the following tutors in university departments and colleges of education who underwent training in the use of the observation schedule and carried out observations within schools. Not only did their time, freely given, enable us thoroughly to test the schedule under classroom conditions, but their comments and helpful criticisms made it possible to refine and facilitate the use of the schedule.

A. Ashman	D. Mackean	D. A. Tawney
J. Baker	J. May	A. Thomas
C. Carré	Miss G. Monger	D. Tomley
R. W. Champeney	C. W. Othen	P. Uzzell
R. W. Crossland	C. V. Platts	Miss E. J. Vinnicombe
R. W. Fairbrother	A. J. G. Pritchard	M. Vokins
J. R. Hall	P. E. Richmond	Miss H. E. Wade
D. G. Holford	I. F. Roberts	E. J. Wenham
D. W. G. Hooper	M. Sayer	Dr R. C. Whitfield
Dr R. Ingle	D. W. Scott	P. A. Whittle
E. Jenkins	J. B. Sellwood	A. Womersley
A. Jennings	C. F. Stoneman	Dr G. Yeoman
Miss J. Ling	Dr C. R. Sutton	

We should also like to thank the schools who participated, their heads, and in particular the teachers and the pupils who underwent observation. Without their willing co-operation there could have been no project.

Our thanks are due to Miss Lesley Warrington for assistance in producing the tables and figures, Brian Harrison for his valuable and critical comments on the script and Mrs Kathleen Revill for typing the script.

We are indebted to the following for permission to include transcripts from film and videotape recordings of science lessons in this book.

Mr J. M. Wilson, Assistant Rector, Grange Academy, Kilmarnock, and Jordanhill College of Education, Glasgow, for the sequences on testing oxygen, nitrogen and carbon dioxide, quoted in the first extract on p. 21 and in the Teacher 2 extracts on pp. 26 and 27. These are taken from *Chemistry by Investigation*, an integrated science lesson presented by Mr Wilson and filmed by Jordanhill College (1970).

Unilever Ltd, for the sequences on testing the reactions of copper when heated, quoted in the second and third extracts on p. 21 and in the Teacher 4 extracts on pp. 29–31. These are taken from *Exploring Chemistry*, a Unilever educational film (1967).

Mr G. Clements and the University of Leicester School of Education, for the sequences on locusts feeding in the Teacher 1 extracts on pp. 26, 27 and 28. These are taken from *Enquiry Methods in Biology Teaching*, Part 1 (taught by J. F. Eggleston at Manor High School, Leicestershire), produced and directed by Mr Clements and filmed by the School of Education (1970).

While the authors have tried to ensure that classroom sequences have been faithfully transcribed, they regret that it has not always been practicable to check again with original film or videotape sources. Any minor discrepancies that may occur in no way affect the basic sense of the exchanges between teacher and pupils, nor the operation of the observation schedule.

Materials for the Science Teaching Observation Schedule

In addition to this report, the Schools Council Project for the Evaluation of Science Teaching Methods has produced three videotapes for the purpose of training observers in the use of the Science Teaching Observation Schedule. These tapes are available on hire, and requests for this service should be directed to the Publications Section, Schools Council, 160 Great Portland Street, London W1N 6LL.

TAPE 1: TRAINING IN MAJOR CATEGORIES AND DETAILED TRAINING IN TEACHER TALK AND ACTIVITY

This gives training in the five major categories of the schedule (see pp. 5–6) and more detailed training in the 'teacher talk' categories—1a, *Teacher asks questions* . . . , 1b, *Teacher makes statements* . . . and 1c, *Teacher directs pupils to sources of information* . . . In each case the videotape shows a lesson extract and the observer is asked to attempt a classification of the activities. The intellectual exchanges in the lesson are then analysed and the correct classification justified.

TAPE 2: DETAILED TRAINING IN PUPIL TALK AND ACTIVITY PLUS PRACTICE EXAMPLES

This gives training in categories 2d, *Pupils seek information* . . . and 2e, *Pupils refer to teacher* . . . The same procedure is followed as on Tape 1. The remaining part of the tape consists of examples of various teaching episodes to enable the observer to practise coding. A correct classification of each episode is provided.

TAPE 3: RELIABILITY TRIAL

This consists of three lesson extracts lasting approximately twenty-one minutes and featuring three teachers of biology, chemistry and physics respectively. Data are available so that a trainee observer may compare his results with those of trained observers.

Training

Where possible, it is recommended that training should take place under the direction of an experienced observer. At present it is envisaged that two training sessions per year will be run at the University of Leicester. Particulars may be obtained from Maurice Galton, University of Leicester School of Education, 21 University Road, Leicester, LE1 2RF.

Where an observer attempts to train himself, the following sequence is recommended:

(i) Learn the two main divisions and five major categories of the observation schedule, and the ten ground rules relating to specific categories.

(ii) View all training portions on Tapes 1 and 2.

(iii) Use the practice examples on Tape 2.

(iv) Review the major categories and the 'questions' section on Tape 1.

(v) Carry out the reliability trial using Tape 3.

1 The Science Teaching Observation Schedule

ORIGIN OF THE SCHEDULE

This observation instrument was developed for use in an evaluation study of science teaching methods. The following account describes the essential features of the instrument and the conditions under which it was developed and used.

Our decision to develop the kind of observational tool here described was based on two prior considerations. The first of these was the recognition that curriculum evaluation studies which emulated classical comparative designs had not been conspicuously successful in demonstrating differences between 'treatment' groups and controls. The second consideration was that, although observation instruments have undergone a period of intensive development in recent years, none of the systems focused on those aspects of teaching which we speculated might be among the more potent determinants of achievement in science.

A comparative approach to curriculum evaluation as advocated by such authors as Scriven[1] is based on an experimental model such as that in Fig. 1 (p. 2). Two alternative curriculum 'packages' may be introduced to two groups of classes or schools assigned randomly to one or other of the packages. The independent variable is the nature of the package. The dependent variables consist of outcomes measured as changes of students' behaviour, i.e. what students can do or do better, and/or their affective response. Where no significant difference has been found between two such groups, we may conclude either that there is no demonstrable difference between the two 'treatments' or that there are defects either in the design of the investigation or in the implementation, or both.

The response of some evaluators has been to abandon this *quasi*-experimental approach as simplistic or fundamentally misconceived in favour of alternative methodologies of a non hypothetico-deductive (see p. 3) character. Others have devoted their energies to devising better measures of achievement. A third reaction is initially to examine this model in order to identify possible defects which might be avoided while retaining a scientific rationale for evaluation.

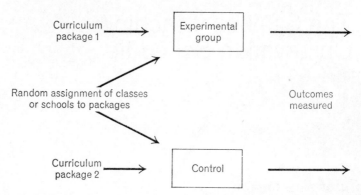

Fig. 1 'Black box' model of the comparative approach to curriculum evaluation

The design illustrated in Fig. 1 includes random assignment of schools or classes to experimental and control groups. The effect of this procedure is to 'equalize' the groups in terms of all possible independent variables so that the single consistent difference between them is the treatment received, i.e. the curriculum package.

This is a 'black box' approach, in the sense that no attention is paid to the mechanisms in the form of teaching tactics (and the participants involved in them) operating in the classes which receive the package. It is possible that these mechanisms might considerably augment or substantially neutralize the effectiveness of the package in achieving whatever outcomes are expected. If there are more potent determinants of achievement or changes of attitude which might be located in pupils, teachers and the transactions taking place between them, then the effect of the package treated in isolation may be so small as to be invisible.

The array of variables which, singly or together, might determine the achievements of some or all pupils, even in the limited context of a science subject, is formidable. The purpose of the Science Teaching Observation Schedule is to describe one subset of variables; to take the lid off the black box and selectively attend to particular events. The schedule is exclusively concerned with some *intellectual transactions* which take place in science lessons. It includes transactions which occur between teachers and pupils, between the pupils themselves, and between pupils and resources.

Before attempting to devise another schedule and thus add to the seventy or so well-documented schedules available, we searched for an instrument which satisfied the following criteria.

(i) It should facilitate the recording of those intellectual behaviours associated with science, e.g. observing, constructing hypotheses, speculating, designing experiments, inferring and so on.

(ii) In some categories of behaviour the schedule should enable fairly detailed records to be made, e.g. different kinds of questions involving different thought processes.

(iii) It should include interaction not only between teachers and pupils, and between the pupils themselves, but also between pupils and resources.

(iv) The record obtained should result in a frequency of use profile on which a typology of teaching styles could be based.

(v) The schedule must be of a kind which could be used by a large team of trained observers who would operate in a large sample of schools.

No instrument currently available satisfied these conditions.

DEVELOPMENT OF THE SCHEDULE

Observation schedules fall into two broad categories. The first category contains those schedules which are wide in their coverage, concerned not only with cognitive and affective events which take place in classrooms, but also with managerial processes and the physical characteristics of the learning environment. The information obtained by the implementation of such schedules yields data which are used to search for patterns in the events taking place in classrooms. Studies of this kind could properly be called *inductive*.

The second category, in contrast, directs the observer's attention to a relatively small specific subset of observable events. Justification for this restriction is sought by reference to hypothesized connexions between these observed events and outcomes (often pupil attainment or attitude measures). Thus, for example, the hypothesis that happy teachers produce contented pupils might justify counting teachers' smiles and relating this to some outcome measure of pupil contentment! Studies of this kind, including all *process–product* studies, are *hypothetico-deductive* in character.

It is sufficient at this point to note that the data made available by observation are frequently reduced to a small number of 'dimensions' which may be used as independent variables in either correlational or experimental researches such as process–product studies. This reduction may occur at the end, as in a truly inductive study, or near the beginning, when models may be borrowed from psychology (e.g. when Gallagher[2] used Guilford's model of the intellect) or newly devised as an explicit formulation of the researcher's perceptions of some learning processes.

The Science Teaching Observation Schedule was designed for use in a kind of process–product study. It directs the observers' attention to intellectual transactions taking place in science lessons. Initially, there was no attempt to use theoretical models borrowed from psychology nor to base the schedule on any explicitly formulated set of parameters. The main guide was the recognition that recent developments in science teaching include an acceptance of the processes of science as an integral part of learning science.

At the outset, observers used trial versions of the schedule in order to determine the extent to which behaviours, accepted as part of the intellectual equipment of students of science, were represented in science classrooms. The schedule was developed through a succession of trials under field conditions in order to achieve the requirements previously described (p. 2). The path taken in the evolution of the schedule was influenced not only by the prerequisite condition that the observation instrument should be reliable in the hands of trained observers, but also by the expectation that it would be possible to establish a typology of teaching styles. That is, we hoped to be able to assign teachers and their classes to categories according to observed features of the intellectual transactions taking place between them.

It follows that our interests centred upon those intellectual transactions which facilitated such a differentiation among teachers and their classes into groups, each designated according to its style. Features common to all or most science classrooms tended progressively to assume less significance.

Four decisions were made during this embryonic phase of the development of the schedule. These may be briefly represented as the answers to the following questions.

(i) Will permanent taped (video or sound) records be kept for later analysis?
(ii) Should a category or sign system be used?
(iii) Which intellectual transactions will be observed?
(iv) At what rate will observations be made and how will the 'universe' of all possible intellectual transactions between a teacher and his class be sampled?

The answer to the first question was 'no', excepting those videotaped records kept for the purpose of training observers. This decision was made on the grounds of cost and because of the many technical difficulties involved. However, the main reason for rejecting permanent taped records was the size of the sample of teachers in whose laboratories and classrooms observation was to take place. This included more than 100 teachers, dispersed from the southwest to the northeast of England.

The second decision concerning the nature of the observation system to be used was resolved in favour of a *sign* system. *Category* systems such as that used by Flanders and Amidon[3,7] contain very broad categories of events, for example 'teacher asks question'. These categories have to be broad to facilitate the near-instant classification of every event taking place in a classroom, in sequence, and at high frequency. The system cited above requires observers to observe and categorize events at three-second intervals. Even 'silence or confusion' is included in the set of categories.

A sign system, on the other hand, does not demand that every event is classified. A selected subset of behaviours is recorded either when one occurs or when it occurs within predetermined time sampling units. Because the Science Teaching Observation Schedule is designed to facilitate a detailed record of specifically intellectual behaviours, a *sign* system was deemed to be more appropriate. It is important to note that a sign system, unlike a category system, does not yield detailed information on the sequence of events as they occur.

A complete answer to the third question, 'which intellectual transactions will be observed?' will be left until the observation schedule is described (see below). Sufficient has been said to indicate that the Science Teaching Observation Schedule is limited to cognitive behaviours observed in the exchanges between teachers and pupils and between the pupils themselves. It is not concerned with affective response or with managerial manoeuvres.

The decisions to use time sampling units of three minutes' duration, and to observe each teacher for approximately four hours, owed more to pragmatism than theory. The first of these decisions was, in effect, a compromise between the most detailed record possible, on the one hand, and the time taken for the observer to perform his tasks of observing, identifying and classifying, on the other. Both decisions rest on the requirement that in order to determine that teacher A and his class belong to a different category from teacher B and his class, it is necessary to show that variation in the use of categories from occasion to occasion by either A or B separately is less than variation between the use by A and B together. Provided the time sampling units are short enough to facilitate such discrimination and long enough for the observers to cope with their task, all is well.

Solutions to the problems of how frequently and how long to observe each teacher were in our research constrained by the cost of observation in terms of both money and time. Our results indicate that observation of about four hours spread over four separate occasions is satisfactory, in so far as it allows classification of teachers and their classes into groups according to predominant features of the 'cognitive' style of interaction (see p. 18, lines 5–7).

THE SCIENCE TEACHING OBSERVATION SCHEDULE

The schedule is a device for classifying and recording certain kinds of events as they occur in science lessons. The classification of these events is organized as follows.

There is a dichotomy into (**1**) those events initiated by the teacher, entitled 'teacher talk' and (**2**) those events initiated and/or maintained by pupils, entitled 'talk and activity initiated and/or maintained by pupils'.

The first of these is divided into three *major categories*:

a Teacher asks questions (or invites comments) which are answered by . . .
b Teacher makes statements . . .
c Teacher directs pupils to sources of information for the purpose of . . .

The second arm of the dichotomy is divided into two major categories:

d   Pupils seek information or consult for the purpose of . . .

e   Pupils refer to teacher for the purpose of . . .

Fig. 2 illustrates the main features of the classification of the subset of observed events.

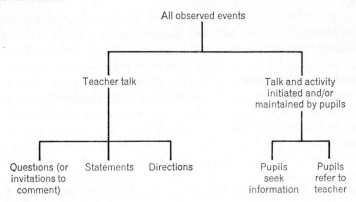

Fig. 2   Main features of the classification used in the Science Teaching Observation Schedule

Each of the five *major* categories **a** to **e** is subdivided into *minor* categories. An attempt has been made to order these minor categories into patterns which facilitate recording. Major category **1a**, *Teacher asks questions (or invites comments) which are answered by* . . . , is subdivided into seven minor categories a_1 to a_7:

a_1 recalling facts and principles;

a_2 applying facts and principles to problem solving;

a_3 making hypothesis or speculation;

a_4 designing of experimental procedure;

a_5 direct observation;

a_6 interpreting of observed or recorded data;

a_7 making inferences from observations or data.

Major category **1b**, *Teacher makes statements* . . . , contains four sub-categories:

b_1 of fact and principle;

b_2 of problems;

b_3 of hypothesis or speculation;

b_4 of experimental procedure.

This pattern is substantially repeated in the succeeding major categories. Thus category **1c**, *Teacher directs pupils to sources of information for the purpose of* . . . , contains the four minor categories:

c_1 acquiring or confirming facts or principles;

c_2 identifying problems;

c_3 making inferences, formulating or testing hypotheses;

c_4 seeking guidance on experimental procedure.

Similarly, in the division concerned with pupil-initiated or pupil-maintained activity, the major category **2d**, *Pupils seek information or consult for the purpose of* . . . , contains the four minor categories:

d_1 acquiring or confirming facts or principles;

d_2 identifying or solving problems;

d_3 making inferences, formulating or testing hypotheses;

d_4 seeking guidance on experimental procedure.

Finally, the major category **2e**, *Pupils refer to teachers for the purpose of* . . . , is similarly sub-categorized into;

e_1 acquiring or confirming facts or principles;

e_2 seeking guidance when identifying or solving problems;

e_3 seeking guidance when making inferences, formulating or testing hypotheses;

e_4 seeking guidance on experimental procedure.

A copy of the complete schedule as used by observers is in Fig. 3 (p. 8).

The columns on the right hand side of the schedule marked 0, 3, 6, 9, 12, etc. represent a continuous series of time sampling units of three minutes' duration which lasts throughout the whole period of observation. A tick is made in a cell when a behaviour identified and classified in a minor category occurs. Only one such entry is made in any time sampling unit, no matter how frequently the behaviour occurred during that time unit. Any number of the twenty-three classified behaviours may occur in any one time sampling unit.

SUGGESTED PROCEDURE FOR USING THE SCHEDULE

Two essential preconditions which we strongly advise should be met are that the observers be trained, and that they establish a good open relationship with the teacher and class to be observed.

It is our experience that, provided the teachers and classes are assured that observation is not judgement, teachers are not threatened by the presence of an observer. We have been surprised by the ease with which observers were assimilated into the learning environment. Nevertheless, it is important to ensure that observations are made of a situation similar to that which obtains in the observer's absence and not of an artefact caused by his presence. Observers should cultivate the confidence of teachers. If teachers wish to see the observation schedule or the record of their performance, there is no reason why they should not do so, but it is desirable that they should do so

Fig. 3 The Science Teaching Observation Schedule

Name of observer . . . .

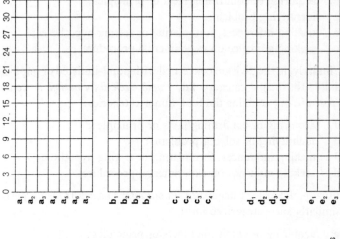

1 TEACHER TALK

1a *Teacher asks questions (or invites comments) which are answered by:*

a_1 recalling facts and principles
a_2 applying facts and principles to problem solving
a_3 making hypothesis or speculation
a_4 designing of experimental procedure
a_5 direct observation
a_6 interpretation of observed or recorded data
a_7 making inferences from observations or data

1b *Teacher makes statements:*

b_1 of fact and principle
b_2 of problems
b_3 of hypothesis or speculation
b_4 of experimental procedure

1c *Teacher directs pupils to sources of information for the purpose of:*

c_1 acquiring or confirming facts or principles
c_2 identifying or solving problems
c_3 making inferences, formulating or testing hypotheses
c_4 seeking guidance on experimental procedure

2 TALK AND ACTIVITY INITIATED AND/OR MAINTAINED BY PUPILS

2d *Pupils seek information or consult for the purpose of:*

d_1 acquiring or confirming facts or principles
d_2 identifying or solving problems
d_3 making inferences, formulating or testing hypotheses
d_4 seeking guidance on experimental procedure

2e *Pupils refer to teacher for the purpose of:*

e_1 acquiring or confirming facts or principles
e_2 seeking guidance when identifying or solving problems
e_3 seeking guidance when making inferences, formulating or testing hypotheses
e_4 seeking guidance on experimental procedure

after the observations are complete. It is also important to try to establish that lessons observed do not constitute 'special' performances—unless, of course, some prescribed 'style' is a feature of an experimental study. The research in which this observation instrument was developed required that the style of teaching observed was typical of that normally used by the teachers and classes involved.

Random visits by observers may be methodologically ideal but are difficult to achieve in practice. One obvious safeguard against including lessons which may have deviated from a teacher's stylistic norm is to ask the teacher if events had conspired to produce such a lesson. The observer has an important part to play: he must not only record accurately the categories of behaviour observed, but also note any gross features of the lesson's organization which might affect the record in such a way as to lead to misinterpretation.

When these conditions are met, the efficient use of the schedule demands that the observer position himself where he can hear what is being said without intruding. There are occasions when the observer may have to change position so as to pick up dialogue within a group or between a teacher and an individual. No rigid procedure is advised. The observer's task is to observe as much of the action as he can.

It is strongly advised that observers should be asked to give an account, on the back of the observation schedule, of any features of the lesson which might have affected the nature of the intellectual transactions which took place in it.

All observers were given the following instructions before beginning the visits to teachers.

You are provided with observation schedules and spare recording sheets. At the end of an observation session, detach the sheet and record on the reverse side your comments on the lesson. These should include:

  (*a*) a brief description on the content and aims of the lesson;
  (*b*) how the lesson worked out;
  (*c*) whether there were particular problems with regard to classroom manage-
       ment which might have unduly influenced the intellectual transactions.

The following report was made during the pilot study stage and is given by way of example.

LESSON—PHYSICS

Aim and content of lesson: Lessons consist of a study of the expansion of metals. Pupils were asked to suggest ways in which different metals could be compared in terms of the amount they expand on heating. By examining the factors that they would need to take into account in order to make such comparisons the pupils are led towards the idea that they need to compare the expansion of a fixed length of metal at a fixed temperature difference. During the next quarter-hour the teacher then shows the pupils the apparatus for measuring expansion and explains the procedure to be adopted in making the measurements. Pupils raised a number of questions concerned with the experiment. For example:

PUPIL   How will we know if it reaches the temperature?
TEACHER   We will give it five minutes.
PUPIL   How will we know if this time is long enough?
TEACHER   You will have to take my word for it.

How the lesson worked out: The experiment had to be repeated three times before it worked correctly. The first time the teacher forgot to measure the initial length of the metal bar. 'Why didn't you stop me?' she asks the class. One girl at the back replies quietly, 'You're the teacher.' After the second occasion, when she forgot to clamp the bar firmly enough, she tells the class to go and copy up the diagram while she repeats the experiment again. With these delays the discussion of results for the various metals is rushed and by the end the teacher is forced to write the formula for the coefficient of expansion on the board. The class is told to copy out the data which she summarizes on the board to calculate the coefficient of expansion for each metal for homework.

Classroom management: On the whole the class was attentive, at least in the early stages, although they became somewhat bored when the experiment had to be repeated more than once. Some of the pupils clearly could have prevented the mistakes if they had chosen to do so but it seemed that the older boys, in particular, tended to regard the teacher as someone other than simply a 'voice of authority' in the classroom, and took delight in trying to put her out of her stride.

In this example, the decision would probably be taken to eliminate the record of the observations as not being typical of the teacher's normal lesson. The need to repeat the experiment not only resulted in a repetitive pattern of events recorded on the schedule, but it also forced this teacher to depart from her strategy of getting the pupils to work out among themselves a method of arriving at some measure of expansivity. In the end she had to write this expression down. Thus the record tended to over-emphasize the use of categories b_1 and c_1 at the expense of pupil-initiated activity

TRAINING

Allied to the observation schedule are the User's Manual (see Chapter 2), two training videotapes and a reliability trial videotape. The manual contains an account of the major and minor categories, gives examples of each in the form of transcripts from lesson sequences, and describes ten rules governing the use of the schedule. The use of the training and reliability trial videotapes is described on p. xiii.

Almost all the forty or so observers trained to use this system in the current research programme were tutors involved in teacher training. They were experienced observers who were, so to speak, 'converted' to the system. This no doubt made a major contribution to the success of a relatively short training programme. These observers were trained during a one-day session prior to which they had been asked to learn the contents of the User's Manual. The training session consisted of informal small group discussion centred on the training tapes.

The arrangement which those undergoing training found acceptable was a division of the day's training into three parts. The first session consisted of a recapitulation of the contents of the schedule and the rules, followed by the beginning of training tape 1, the major categories, and the 'questions' sequence from the minor categories, also on tape 1. The second session consisted of the remainder of training tapes 1 and 2; this was followed by session three, the reliability trial, with tape 3.

It is important to ensure that the day's training is interspersed with periods for relaxation to avoid fatigue.

RELIABILITY

Since the schedule was to be used by forty observers, it was necessary to provide a way of checking on the reliability of this group that did not require the research team to accompany each observer during his visits to various teachers. Accordingly, a reliability tape, consisting of extracts taken from three lessons involving different teachers, was constructed. The extracts were chosen to represent teachers with contrasting styles including as many of the activities described by the schedule as possible. Obviously there were limits to achieving the latter requirement. In all, two reliability trial videotapes were produced. The first reliability tape consisted of three nine-minute sequences. This was seen by all observers immediately after training. It proved unsatisfactory, however, because it was not possible to cover all the minor categories within the twenty-seven minutes of film, and also because one of the film sequences proved difficult to interpret unambiguously without making assumptions as to what was taking place outside the view of the television camera. Subsequently a second reliability tape was made with three extracts lasting twenty-one minutes each, giving a total of twenty-one time sampling units. This was shown to twenty-one observers who attended a retraining session. It is the data from this second tape which provide the basis of the analysis given below.

In computing the reliability of an observation schedule, two methods are usually applied. The first simply calculates the extent of the agreement between any two observers, using a variety of coefficients such as chi squared[4] or product–moment correlation,[5] or those based upon the use of the binomial model such as the Scott coefficient.[6–8] In the second method, preferred by Medley and Mitzel,[4,8] the scores of all observers on their visits to various teachers over a number of occasions are pooled and a two-way analysis of variance is performed. In this analysis the teacher variation is regarded as an estimate of the 'true' variance and the reliability coefficient indicates how well the group of observers is able to discriminate between various teachers

Table 1 Coefficients of agreement for twenty-one observers using the schedule

Observation category	Observer (A)	(B)	(C)	(D)	(E)	(F)	(G)	(H)	(I)	(J)
a_1	0·52	0·62	0·71	0·62	0·81	0·61	0·24	0·52	0·71	0·64
a_2	0·42	0·43	0·91	0·62	0·62	0·91	0·24	0·81	0·52	0·08
a_3	0·71	0·52	0·81	0·81	0·91	0·81	0·81	0·62	0·71	0·81
a_4	0·42	0·62	0·71	0·52	0·81	0·62	0·43	0·80	0·62	0·33
a_5	0·61	0·91	0·71	0·52	0·81	0·81	0·63	0·80	0·71	0·71
a_6	0·81	0·81	0·81	0·81	0·72	0·43	0·81	0·62	0·71	0·55
a_7	0·33	0·61	0·52	0·62	0·62	0·43	0·33	0·45	0·33	0·62
b_1	1·00	0·33	0·43	0·24	0·72	0·52	0·24	0·52	0·91	0·43
b_2	0·71	0·71	0·71	0·24	0·52	0·71	0·61	0·62	0·81	0·52
b_3	0·95	0·91	0·81	1·00	1·00	1·00	0·71	0·81	0·42	1·00
b_4	0·62	0·43	0·62	0·52	0·61	0·62	0·45	0·81	0·62	0·43
c_1	0·05	0·33	0·42	0·33	0·24	0·52	0·14	0·33	0·43	0·33
c_2	0·71	0·91	1·00	0·91	0·81	0·91	0·71	0·91	0·81	0·81
c_3	1·00	1·00	1·00	0·72	1·00	1·00	1·00	0·71	0·81	1·00
c_4	0·91	1·00	0·52	0·91	1·00	1·00	0·71	0·91	0·91	0·90
d_1	0·33	0·43	0·33	0·43	0·15	0·52	0·33	0·42	0·62	0·52
d_2	0·90	0·91	0·71	1·00	0·81	0·90	1·00	0·91	0·81	0·70
d_3	0·90	0·91	0·91	1·00	1·00	0·90	0·91	0·91	0·81	1·00
d_4	0·90	0·91	1·00	1·00	0·91	1·00	0·91	1·00	0·91	0·90
e_1	0·61	0·81	0·81	0·62	0·71	0·81	0·72	0·62	0·81	0·71
e_2	0·81	0·91	0·91	0·92	0·52	1·00	0·62	0·91	0·71	1·00
e_3	0·71	0·71	0·81	0·71	0·71	0·81	1·00	0·71	0·91	0·71
e_4	0·91	0·91	0·74	0·71	0·91	0·81	0·52	0·91	0·81	0·91

Note
The table gives the coefficients of agreement obtained from twenty-one observers whose records were compared with those of the team. In categories where, in the team's judgement, the activity occurred rarely, agreement is usually very high, as in categories c_3, c_4, d_2, d_3 and d_4. These high values arise because it is easier for an observer to recognize the absence of activity rather than identify the appropriate behaviour code once it has taken place.

(K)	(L)	(M)	(N)	(O)	(P)	(Q)	(R)	(S)	T)	(U)
0·62	0·62	0·53	0·43	0·43	0·33	0·24	0·45	0·62	0·25	0·75
0·33	0·43	0·62	0·52	0·53	0·33	0·33	0·62	0·91	0·52	0·45
0·52	0·92	0·53	1·00	0·62	0·81	0·81	0·52	0·81	0·62	0·71
0·52	0·61	0·42	0·62	0·62	0·52	0·71	0·62	0·55	0·25	0·62
0·81	0·81	0·71	0·62	0·63	0·52	0·55	0·42	0·71	0·71	0·52
0·62	0·62	0·81	0·42	0·81	0·62	0·62	0·45	0·92	0·33	0·81
0·53	0·62	0·52	0·52	0·45	0·52	0·62	0·62	0·62	0·72	0·74
0·62	0·43	0·63	0·71	0·81	0·05	0·14	0·33	0·33	0·54	0·33
0·91	0·55	0·81	0·33	0·52	0·81	0·71	0·33	0·72	0·45	0·81
0·52	0·90	1·00	1·00	0·81	1·00	0·91	0·81	1·00	1·00	1·00
0·72	0·24	0·29	0·24	0.40	0·52	0·62	0·62	0·62	0·71	0·24
0·33	0·33	0·33	0·62	0·52	0·43	0·71	0·24	0·33	0·62	0·42
0·81	0·62	0·71	0·81	0·71	1·00	0·91	0·44	0·82	0·93	0·71
1·00	0·91	1·00	1·00	1·00	1·00	1·00	0·91	0·92	1·00	0·91
1·00	0·91	0·905	0·90	1·00	1·00	1·00	1·00	1·00	1·00	0·81
0·33	0·33	0·61	0·45	0·33	0·52	0·62	0·33	0·43	0·45	0·55
1·00	0·71	0·62	0·91	0·90	0·91	0·91	1·00	0·81	0·90	0·92
1·00	0·90	0·71	1·00	1·00	0·91	1·00	1·00	0·92	0·91	1 00
1·00	1·00	0·81	1·00	0·91	1·00	1·00	1·00	1·00	1·00	0·81
0·81	0·81	0·81	0·62	0·81	0·81	0·72	0·91	0·90	0·82	0·62
0·81	0·81	0·81	0·90	0·91	0·90	0·80	0·81	0·90	0·90	0·81
0·81	0·71	0·71	0·81	0·71	0·72	0·81	0·72	0·71	0·72	0·71
0·80	0·55	0·92	0·91	0·90	0·81	0·80	0·90	0·85	0·91	1·00

Categories b_1, c_1 and d_1 provide the lowest agreement, and indicate that observers who miscoded c_1 usually placed the tick in b_1, thus affecting scores on both categories. This low agreement stems from the difficulty of using Rule 10 (p. 23) to distinguish between categories c and b when videotape is used. An individual observer's overall performance can be assessed by averaging the coefficient of agreement over all categories. While this is only an approximate measure, it serves to indicate a need for further training.

over each category. In examining the reliability tape data there are good reasons for obtaining values for both the inter-observer agreement, based on comparison between each observer's score and the coding of the tape by the research team, and also a group reliability. The latter is an estimate of the extent to which the whole group of observers discriminates between the three film episodes of the different teachers over the twenty-three minor categories of the schedule.

Coefficient of agreement
A simple coefficient of agreement, R_a, can be obtained from the expression:

$$R_a = \frac{(a+d)-(b+c)}{(a+b+c+d)}$$

where $a =$ the number of occasions when the category was judged to be used by both the team and the observer;

$b =$ the number of occasions when the category was judged to be used by the team but not the observer;

$c =$ the number of occasions when the category was judged to be used by the observer but not by the team;

$d =$ the number of occasions when both the team and the observer judged that the category was not used.

This coefficient of agreement is not completely satisfactory, first, because without a knowledge of the sampling distribution of the coefficient there is no way of determining the significance of a particular value, and secondly, because it depends on the total number of time sampling units observed. In this case, with only twenty-one time sampling units, for each disagreement between the team and observer, the coefficient is reduced by about 5%. Table 1 (p. 12) gives the coefficient of agreement matrix for the twenty-one observers over the twenty-three minor categories of the observation schedule. In assessing the data it must be remembered that the schedule aims to classify a sample of teachers according to the frequency with which they and their class engage in specified activities, when compared to the population of teachers who undergo observation. In discriminating between teaching styles, a teacher's score is obtained by adding the ticks obtained in each time sampling unit to arrive at a composite score for a category. Thus it is not necessary that observers should agree on the exact time unit in which the activity occurred, provided that the relative proportion of ticks given to different teachers is the same for each observer. The coefficient of agreement which determines the extent to which observers agree about what happened *in a particular time unit* does not always have to be near the 0·9 mark. Provided observers can be shown to operate the schedule consistently as a group (this aspect is dealt with in the second part of the analysis, concerning group reliability, below) lower levels of agreement are acceptable. It is usual to regard values of the order of 0·6 as satisfactory.

Judged in the light of the above, much of the data is satisfactory. The most difficult categories in which to secure agreement would appear from Table 1 to be a_2 and a_7 in the questions and b_1, c_1 and d_1 in the remaining sections. The difficulty of observers in using a_2, *applying facts and principles to problem solving*, and a_7, *making inferences from observations or data*, has consistently arisen during trials of the schedule and was also a feature of the initial reliability trial. Since there is a sequential relationship between the two, problem solving usually being preceded by inference, it is not surprising that observers find difficulty in applying the ground rules (given in Chapter 2, User's Manual) designed to enable them to separate these two activities. In the final resort it may be necessary to combine the two categories in one. When this was done during the first reliability trial (see p. 11), an average agreement of between 0·3 and 0·4 for the two categories when separate was increased to 0·65 when they were combined. At this stage in the development of the schedule, however, we preferred to leave the two categories separate and carry out the combining procedure during the subsequent analysis.

The low values for b_1, c_1 and d_1 arise from a different source of error. Experience indicates that category b_1, *teacher makes statements of fact and principle*, is the easiest of all categories for an observer to recognize. It is also the most frequently occurring one. The difficulty here almost certainly arises from the problem associated with category c_1, *teacher directs pupils to sources of information for the purpose of acquiring or confirming facts or principles*. In the ground rules such directives are recorded only if the pupils subsequently act upon the directives. In class, for example, if a teacher tells pupils to 'write something down', it is easy for the observer to reach a decision whether to tick c_1 since he can see if the pupils are writing down this 'something'. Using filmed episodes where the camera tends to concentrate on individuals, it is often more difficult to decide if the teacher's directive has been carried out.

Associated with the use of c_1 are two more ground rules which require unachieved directives to be placed in b_1, and the continuing activity resulting from the directive to be recorded as d_1 in subsequent time units. Consequently, failure to agree on a c_1 activity will almost certainly result in further disagreement in both b_1 and d_1. This is what took place here, since the team tended to interpret these rules concerning pupil participation much more rigidly than the observers. However, in the classroom much of the source of this difficulty might reasonably be expected to disappear.

Group reliability

The analysis of variance design used by Medley and Mitzel[4,8] must be modified because there is no replication of a teacher's score over several occasions. The total variation of scores for all observers with respect to a particular category may thus be partitioned between that due to the teacher, s_t, and s_r the variation remaining. This latter may be regarded as being due to a number of sources of error, including differences between observers. In our model both the teachers and the observers are regarded as 'fixed', i.e. they are not regarded as a sample from a larger population, so that the group reliability, R_c, is given by:

$$R_c = \frac{s_t - s_r}{s_t}$$

A prerequisite of the calculation of reliability is that the F-ratio s_t/s_r should be significant (the level was set at 1%). Failure to reach this level could be due either to disagreement between observers or, as is more usually the case, because the use of a particular category is not sufficient to discriminate effectively between teachers.

The group reliability values for 21 of the 23 categories of the observation schedule are given in Table 2. The data are very satisfactory, confirming the results of the first reliability trial, involving all the observers, that the group as a whole use the observation schedule in a consistent manner. The poor value for c_1 reinforces the earlier conclusion that observers had difficulty not only in agreeing with the research team but also in agreeing among themselves in using this category.

Table 2 Measures of group reliability for twenty-one observers using the schedule

Questions							
Category	a_1	a_2	a_3	a_4	a_5	a_6	a_7
R_c	0·904	0·870	0·947	0·987	0·991	0·987	0·985
Statements and directives							
Category	b_1	b_2	b_3	b_4	c_1	c_2	c_3
R_c	09·79	0·933	0·854	0·993	0·508	0·635	0·804
Pupil activity							
Category	d_1	d_2	d_3	d_4	e_1	e_2	e_3
R_c	0·838	0·922	0·959	0·968	0·983	0·908	0·888

Note: Categories c_4 and e_4 are omitted. Sufficient examples could not be found on the training film to ensure adequate between-teacher variation, so that F-ratio s_t/s_r was not significant.

SUBSEQUENT USE OF THE SCHEDULE

The observers have since had an opportunity to use the schedule in a variety of class settings, observing each of four teachers on four occasions. The total number of observation hours recorded is over 300 which, in terms of use, is in advance of any other corresponding interaction analysis system. Preliminary analysis shows that a teacher with a particular class appears to be consistent in the use of most of the categories over a wide range of content, but more detailed study is now taking place with a view to exploring the inconsistencies. It may be, for example, that where a teacher gives a single period 'theory' lesson followed by a double period of practical work, based upon previous theory, both lessons should be treated as a single occasion for purposes of analysis. A further study involves a group of six observers, including the research team, each visiting the same teacher on different occasions. This is designed to examine the consistency of teachers in more detail.

References

1   M. Scriven. 'The methodology of evaluation', in R. W. Tyler, R. M. Gagné and M. Scriven, *Perspectives of Curriculum Evaluation* (American Educational Research Association Monograph on Curriculum Evaluation no. 1). Chicago: Rand McNally, 1967.
2   J. J. Gallagher. 'A "topic classification system" for classroom interaction', in J. J. Gallagher, G. A. Nuthall and B. Rosenshine, *Classroom Observation* (American Educational Research Association Monograph on Curriculum Evaluation no. 6). Chicago: Rand McNally, 1970.
3   N. A. Flanders. *Teacher Influences, Pupil Attitudes and Achievement* (Cooperative Research Monograph no. 12). US Department of Health, Education and Welfare, 1965.
4   D. M. Medley and H. E. Mitzel. 'Measuring classroom behavior by systematic observation', in *Handbook of Research on Teaching*, ed. N. L. Gage. Chicago: Rand McNally, 1963, pp. 247–328.
5   F. G. Cornell, C. M. Lindvall and J. L. Saupe. *An Exploratory Measure of Individualities of Schools and Classrooms*. Urbana, Illinois: Bureau of Educational Research, University of Illinois, 1952.
6   W. A. Scott. 'Reliability of content analysis: the case of nominal scale coding', *Public Opinion Quarterly*, **19**, 1955, 321–5.
7   N. A. Flanders. 'The problems of observer training and reliability', in *Interaction Analysis: Theory, Research and Application*, ed. E. J. Amidon and B. J. Hough. Reading, Massachusetts: Addison-Wesley, 1967, pp. 158–66.
8   D. M. Medley and H. E. Mitzel. 'Application of analysis of variance to the estimation of the reliability of observation of teachers' classroom behavior', *Journal of Experimental Education*, **27**, 1, 1958, 23–35.

2 User's manual

INTRODUCTION

The purpose of the Science Teaching Observation Schedule is to enable observers to record accurately a selection of intellectual transactions which take place between pupils and teachers in science lessons. The schedule can be used in lessons where the major component is theoretical as well as in laboratory-based work. The final product of the schedule is an estimate of the probability that certain kinds of intellectual transactions are used by a teacher and these constitute what might be referred to as his cognitive style. The range of intellectual transactions which are included in this schedule cover, for example, the kinds of statement that the teacher makes, the kinds of question he asks, and the types of direction he gives. The pupils' reactions to these teacher behaviours are also recorded in the schedule. Thus if, pupils refer to sources of information, such activities are recorded in categories according to the purpose served by the reference, for example, testing hypotheses. In order to illustrate the categories in this observation schedule, the project has made videotape recordings of extracts from science lessons, containing examples of teacher–pupil interaction which may be classified in the categories used (see description of Tapes 1 and 2 on p. xii). It is important to read this manual before consulting the videotapes.

This schedule has been designed primarily for use by observers present at the lesson as it takes place. It may also be used to classify teacher–pupil interaction as recorded on videotape, or even as transcribed from audio tape, but in these cases the restricted nature of the information available could lead to errors of classification.

SAMPLING AND SCORING

The scores obtained from the schedule will be used to classify teachers on the basis of their teaching style. One only needs to record a sample of a selected number of behaviours which can be shown to discriminate effectively between teachers using different styles. Thus it is not necessary to record every verbal communication which takes place in the course of a lesson.

The manner of scoring is as follows. Whenever an observer considers that a particular behaviour which is specified in the schedule has occurred, he places a tick in the particular category. The whole lesson is divided up into three-minute time units. Having recorded a particular category within a three-minute period, no further reference to it is made until the next time unit commences. *No category can therefore be ticked more than once during any time unit.* At the end of the lesson the observer adds up the number of ticks which have occurred for each category, and these totals are then recorded on a separate sheet.

In assigning particular behaviours to particular categories, the observer will have to make certain on-the-spot decisions. To make this task as easy as possible, and to facilitate rapid recording of the behaviour, a number of ground rules have been developed.

Rule 1   Each behaviour is recorded once only during any time unit, no matter how frequently it actually occurs in this time.

Rule 2   Where the behaviour to be recorded extends across the boundary between two adjacent time units, the appropriate category is recorded in both time units.

Rule 3   Where there is some doubt as to the category in which a particular behaviour should be placed, record the most dominant one. If it is not possible to distinguish the most dominant category, then record all categories in which the behaviour is thought to occur.

GENERALIZED DESCRIPTIONS OF THE SCHEDULE

A full set of categories is shown in the earlier description of the instrument (Fig. 3, p. 8). In seeking to classify a particular behaviour, the observer first asks himself two questions.

Question one: Is the behaviour predominantly teacher activity or is it initiated or maintained by the pupil?

A problem which arises in some cases involves a situation where the teacher has previously given a direction to the pupils. He may, for example, say 'Get into groups and discuss this amongst yourselves.' The discussion may, however, take up to ten minutes of the lesson time, and there is clearly some point at which it ceases to be teacher-directed and continues only because of the activities of the pupils. Such cases are covered under Rule 4.

Rule 4   Where a teacher's direction results in pupils engaging in some form of talk or activity, if this pupil behaviour extends beyond the time unit in which the directive is recorded, it should subsequently be classified under pupil-initiated talk or activity.

Having decided whether the talk or activity is teacher-centred or pupil-centred, the observer then considers the major subdivisions within each part of the schedule. If, for example, he has determined that the behaviour involves teacher activity, he will ask:

Question two: Is the teacher asking questions, making statements or giving directives?

We will now consider each one of these in turn.

1a   *Teacher asks questions (or invites comments) which are answered by . . .*
Having decided that the behaviour is a question, the observer then attempts to place it in one of the seven categories. The exact category to be used can only be decided in terms of which pupils' response the teacher is prepared to accept. Often the teacher, when he receives an answer which he regards as unsatisfactory, will by subsequent questioning make it clear what he had in mind when he asked the original question. In such cases it is the whole episode rather than each individual question which should be used to determine the correct category. One other type of question also occurs—that posed as a rhetorical question. This is covered by Rule 5.

Rule 5   When the teacher asks pupils a question and continues the lesson without waiting for an answer, then such questions are to be classified as statements.

(a_1) *Recalling facts and principles:* Such questions are relatively straightforward. They include such examples as 'what is the name of . . . ?' 'what is the relationship between . . . ?' etc.

(a_2) *Applying facts and principles to problem solving,* (a_3) *making hypothesis or speculation,* (a_7) *making inferences from observations or data:* These three categories are best considered together as they overlap to a certain degree. Such questions most frequently either follow the presentation of previously observed or recorded data, or take place during periods of observation in the course of a lesson. Key words in such questions are 'account for', 'what does this tell us?' or 'explain'. In each case the teacher presents a novel situation to the pupils and asks them for explanations. To distinguish between the three categories, the observer should apply the following rules.

Rule 6   If a novel situation is posed in such a way that the teacher asks for a particular solution or indicates that there is only one particular solution he is prepared to accept, then category a_2 is used.

If, on the other hand, the teacher indicates either that there is more than one solution or that he is prepared to consider alternatives in order to seek the correct answer, then the observer applies Rule 7.

Rule 7   Where solutions to problems can deduced directly from the data provided, then category a_7 is used. When these explanations cannot be tested immediately against the data available and must be established by reference to further investigations, then the behaviour is placed in category a_3.

Two examples which illustrate the use of Rules 6 and 7 are as follows:

TEACHER On the board we have written down the results of two tests. Now then, which one of these do you think can be used to indicate the presence of oxygen?

Applying Rule 6, it is clear that there is a unique solution to this problem. Category a_2 is used.

TEACHER [To boy who is heating a piece of copper in a bunsen flame] What do you think is happening then?
PUPIL I think that something in the flame is doing something to the copper.

Application of Rule 6 here clearly indicates that the question is open-ended and therefore several explanations are possible. Application of Rule 7 indicates that the pupil's explanation must subsequently be verified by further experiment. Category a_3 is used.

Same teacher to another pupil:

TEACHER What do you think is happening then?
PUPIL A black powder is forming *from* the copper.
TEACHER How do you know it is coming from the copper?
PUPIL Because it's [i.e. the copper] got thinner.

This example illustrates two important points in the use of the coding procedure. First, it is the pupil's response rather than the actual form of the question which largely determines the appropriate category. (Notice that the form of the instruction in the schedule is *Teacher asks questions . . . WHICH ARE ANSWERED BY . . .*) Secondly, both the questions and the responses must be included in the sequence in order to extract the full meaning from the exchange. Preliminary inspection would appear to indicate that the pupil was reporting what he had seen when the copper was placed in the bunsen flame. However, the teacher's second question concentrates attention on the phrase 'from the copper' in the pupil's initial reply, and it becomes clear from the teacher's second question and the pupil's answer, 'Because it's got thinner', that the pupil has in fact deduced from the observations that the copper is taking part in a reaction. The pupils' explanation is therefore based upon the evidence he has acquired during his observations, and application of Rule 7 indicates that category a_7 should be used to classify this sequence.

(a_4) *Designing of experimental procedure:* Such questions usually arise after pupils have previously attempted to solve problems or suggest hypotheses. Often the form of the question is 'how did you . . .?' (recall) or 'how would you do that?' where the 'that' is a description involving some experimental procedure. In all such cases, if in the pupil's reply there is an element of designing experiments or applying practical techniques, either for confirming a previous explanation or for testing a suggested hypothesis, then category a_4 is to be used.

(a_5) *Direct observation*, (a_6) *interpretation of observed or recorded data:* These two categories may conveniently be taken together. All questions which do not relate to information obtained either from teacher or pupil observation *during the course of the lesson* or from other sources such as photographs, which depict observations, are excluded from a_5. Cases involving such observations are distinguished by the application of Rule 8.

> **Rule 8**   When the pupil answers a question or makes a comment based on observation and the reply is limited so that the teacher needs to seek no further clarification of the answer, category a_5 is used. In all other cases the question is placed in a_6.

The essential distinction, therefore, is that a_5 relates to a direct description of what the pupil sees. Examples would include such questions as 'has the liquid changed colour?' or 'how many sides does the crystal have?' The use of category a_6, however, involves a more generalized description, in which the pupil needs to organize his perceptions of what he observes before he can give a more extensive account of his observations in what are substantially his own words. (See also the Note to Rule 8, p. 32.)

1b   *Teacher makes statements . . .*
This area is divided into four categories. Each relates quite closely to the first four categories in the 'questions' sequence, and the distinctions to be applied in defining their differences are the same as those already described. One difficulty in classifying statements arises in the case where the teacher is summarizing or recapitulating from earlier lessons, or from an earlier part of the lesson under observation. Such cases will involve the use of Rule 9.

> **Rule 9**   When the teacher, for the purpose of reinforcement, either re-states or summarizes any pupil statement, then category b_1 must be used.

The purpose of this rule may be seen in the case where the teacher, in the course of the lesson, asks questions which result in pupils suggesting a number of hypotheses. Later on in the lesson, the teacher re-states these hypotheses in order to develop procedures for testing them. Although, therefore, his statement is in fact a statement of hypothesis which would normally be included under b_3, in this case, because he has merely summarized the ideas of his pupils, it is classified under b_1.

1c   *Teacher directs pupils to sources of information for the purpose of . . .*
Sources of information are to be classed as books, objects or phenomena, or even other pupils. Directives usually involve some use of the imperative. A

problem may arise involving the use of diagrams or data which the teacher records on the blackboard during the lesson. In the absence of a positive directive, Rule 10 can be applied.

Rule 10   Where the teacher, in the course of a lesson, makes statements to the whole class which are illustrated by drawings, sketches or other illustrative material, then categories b_1 to b_3 are to be used. On the other hand, where illustrative material including blackboard diagrams is used as a source of information to which pupils make extended reference unaccompanied by teacher comments, then **c** categories followed by **d** categories are used.

The distinction here usually involves such cases where the teacher puts material or information on to the board and then requires the class to copy it. During this activity, he may in fact continue with further explanation—a form of running commentary—while the pupils are engaged in copying out the information provided. In such cases, the observer records the activities under teacher statements (**1b**). If, however, the pupils copy out the information and during the course of this activity there are only occasional teacher comments, then the teacher directs (**1c**) category is used, and should the activity extend over two time sampling units, the behaviour changes to pupil-maintained (**2d**). In cases where it proves extremely difficult for the observer to determine the dominant behaviour, he should invoke Rule 3 and record in both categories.

In all cases, behaviours are classified as directives only if there is good evidence that *the pupils act* upon them. This often requires the observer to wait until subsequent pupil activity confirms that the teacher's instructions are being carried out. As in the questioning categories, it is the pupil's *interpretation* rather than the teacher's *intention* which determines the purpose of such directives. For example, the teacher may tell pupils to have a discussion among themselves for the purpose of 'solving' problems which have come to light during an experiment. The observer, listening in to the pupils' conversation, may discover that the exchanges are mainly restricted to confirming or recalling the observations made during the practical work. Such activity would be recorded as c_1 and not c_2.

The above considerations point to a need for observers to delay recording directives until further pupil behaviour confirms the most suitable category. Observers are advised to pencil in a faint question mark in those categories in which they think the activity might be classified at the time of the initial teacher behaviour. They are thus reminded to return and place the tick in one of these categories when they are finally in a position to confirm the status of the activity.

Directives which are given either at the beginning of a lesson (e.g. 'sit down') or during it (e.g. 'shut up') to maintain order, etc. are unrecorded.

2d *Pupils seek information or consult for the purpose of . . .*
This section has four categories, again defined in the light of the earlier ground rules. The appropriate classification is determined by the purpose to which the pupils put the information. Sources of information in this case can of course be books, diagrams on the board, photographs or even other pupils.

2e *Pupils refer to teacher for the purpose of . . .*
This category includes all cases where the pupil, by raising his hand without being asked or by direct intervention, initiates discussion with the teacher. Included under *seeking guidance* (e_2 and e_3) are those instances where the pupil seeks reassurance or approbation for some conclusion or idea. In these cases, the clue to the classification is usually to be found in the response of the teacher. The teacher may say 'good', 'well done' or 'that's right', or some other approving statement.

SUMMARY OF RULES TO BE APPLIED WHEN USING THE SCHEDULE

Before going on to consider examples of teacher–pupil interaction which illustrate the use of each category in the observation schedule, the various rules will now be collected together to facilitate their use. It is hoped that, before passing on to the videotapes, each observer will commit to memory the various ground rules and will thus be able to use the category system without continual reference to the manual.

Method of coding—Rule 1: Each behaviour is recorded once only during any time unit, no matter how frequently it actually occurs in this time.

Behaviours extending across time boundaries—Rule 2: Where the behaviour to be recorded extends across the boundary between two adjacent time units, the appropriate category is recorded in both time units.

Overlap of categories—Rule 3: Where there is some doubt as to the category in which a particular behaviour should be placed, record the most dominant one. If it is not possible to distinguish the most dominant category, then record all categories in which the behaviour is thought to occur.

Relationship of teacher directives and subsequent pupil-initiated activity—Rule 4: Where a teacher's direction results in pupils engaging in some form of talk or activity, if this pupil behaviour extends beyond the time unit in which the directive is recorded, it should subsequently be classified under pupil-initiated talk or activity.

Rhetorical questions—Rule 5: When the teacher asks pupils a question and continues the lesson without waiting for an answer, then such questions are to be classified as statements.

Definition of problems—Rule 6: If a novel situation is posed in such a way that the teacher asks for a particular solution or indicates that there is only one particular solution he is prepared to accept, then category a_2 is used.

Distinction between hypothesizing and inferring—Rule 7: Where solutions to problems can be deduced directly from the data provided, then category a_7 is used. When these explanations cannot be tested immediately against the data available and must be established by reference to further investigations, then the behaviour is placed in category a_3.

Distinction between direct observation and interpretation—Rule 8: When the pupil answers a question or makes a comment based on observation and the reply is limited so that the teacher needs to seek no further clarification of the answer, category a_5 is used. In all other cases, the question is placed in a_6.

Recapitulation of pupil statements—Rule 9: When the teacher, for the purpose of reinforcement, either re-states or summarizes any pupil statement, then category b_1 must be used.

Use of blackboard or diagram—Rule 10: Where the teacher, in the course of a lesson, makes statements to the whole class which are illustrated by drawings, sketches or other illustrative material, then categories b_1 to b_3 are to be used. On the other hand, where illustrative material including blackboard diagrams is used as a source of information to which pupils make extended reference unaccomapnied by teacher comments, then c categories followed by d categories are used.

EXAMPLES OF THE USE OF CATEGORIES

There now follow some examples from four lesson sequences, which are also drawn on to illustrate the training and practice videotapes. Lesson 1, taught by Teacher 1, covers the process of digestion (source: *Enquiry Methods in Biology Teaching*, Part 1 (Manor House School, Univ. of Leicester School of Education, 1970). Lesson 2, involving Teacher 2, is an integrated science lesson in which the properties of nitrogen, oxygen and carbon dioxide are being tested (source: *Chemistry by Investigation*, presenter J. M. Wilson, Jordanhill College of Education, 1970); the examples for categories e_1 to e_3 are based on Teacher 2's style but fictitious, since no actual examples were available for these categories. Lesson 3 with Teacher 3, deals with the growth and properties of crystals; again the dialogue is fictitious. Lesson 4, involving Teacher 4, deals with the nature of the reaction when copper is heated in air (source: *Exploring Chemistry*, Unilever, 1967).

The purpose of these examples is to illustrate the use of the ground rules and to help observers become familiar with the various categories. It is the general experience of those who undergo training that too detailed a study of such examples at this stage can prove counter-productive, since the analysis breaks down the structure of some episodes in far greater detail than would be possible under classroom conditions. Such analysis is best carried out after the first viewing of the training tapes when various filmed examples of teaching are viewed.

Observers are reminded that, under classroom conditions, difficult decisions of classification are often resolved because a more obvious example of the category under consideration manifests itself within the same time sampling unit. The observer is thus able to risk the category without further hesitation.

1a   *Teacher asks questions (or invites comments) which are answered by . . .*

(**a₁**) *Recalling facts and principles*

TEACHER 1   These blood vessels round the intestine, where were they? Where was the richest blood supply?
PUPIL   In the small intestine.

(**a₂**) *Applying facts and principles to problem solving*

TEACHER 2   I've got two jars here, two little tubes with no label on. Start thinking. We've only got two tubes. Can you think of two tests we could do to find out which of these three gases is in these two tubes? It's the same, I know that, it's the same gas in each tube, but I don't know which one. Could you think of two tests which could tell us perhaps which of the gases it was?

(**a₃**) *Making hypothesis or speculation*

TEACHER 1   Now notice how even this cut is [examining locusts feeding in jars]. I wonder what decides whether it cuts exactly this much every time it takes a bite, as it were. You see, for it to be as regular as this, the cut being the same depth all the way along, how do you think that was organized?
PUPIL   Has it got something to do with the palps?

(**a₄**) *Designing of experimental procedure*

TEACHER 3   Look here, you've got this crystal and it's so small you would need a microscope to look at the shape. You've not got one so what are you going to do about it?
PUPIL   Grow it.
TEACHER 3   Well then, how are you going to do that?
PUPIL   First we'd get a saturated solution . . .

(**a₅**) *Direct observation*

TEACHER 2   But what happened when you poured the lime water in there . . . It changed to what? . . . What would you say?
PUPIL   Kind of blue.

(**a₆**) *Interpretation of observed or recorded data*

TEACHER 3   Here's a graph showing the solubility of potash alum at different temperatures. Tell me then, how much salt will you need for a saturated solution at room temperature?
PUPIL   A little over . . .

(**a₇**) *Making inferences from observations or data*

TEACHER 2   We're said already that we don't think number four is much use as a test. What about number one? Well, would you use that as a test to distinguish these? What do you think, Ronald?

PUPIL   Sir, you could use it in some but in others you could not.

TEACHER 2   You could use it in some but not others. You certainly could not tell whether it was carbon dioxide or nitrogen. Mm?

1b *Teacher makes statements . . .*

(**b**₁) *Of fact and principle*

TEACHER 1   Right, if you will look at the board you can see my version. You'll notice it's a sort of scientist's impression and not an artist's impression [a drawing of the mouse digestion system]. The idea was to make what we had discovered and agreed upon as clear as possible. I have just now introduced the names, so let's try and get used to them. The tube that leads through the thorax from the mouth to the stomach is called the oesophagus. Don't ask me why . . .

(**b**₂) *Of problems*

TEACHER 1   This is the problem we have got, therefore. How are fish and chips or other food material changed into the kind of substances which can apparently help a big toe or any other part of your body to grow?

(**b**₃) *Of hypothesis or speculation*

TEACHER 1   Either this is where most of the digestion is or there is another possibility, that this is where . . . what else might be happening? Come on, it follows . . . what happens to it?

PUPIL ——

TEACHER 1   Perhaps, perhaps that's . . . it could be either where the digestion is going on mainly, or it could be where most of the absorption is going on. In other words, where the somewhat, I suppose, changed fish and chips will pass through the alimentary canal into the bloodstream. We don't know, but the rich blood supply rather suggests that this is what might be happening.

(**b**₄) *Of experimental procedure*

TEACHER 2   . . . these tubes. It says it's to hold the jar upside down, so you will have to turn the tube upside down and hold it with its neck under water. Now you must get the open neck under water before you pull the bung out, or of course the gas inside, whatever it is, will mix up with the gas in the room.

1c *Teacher directs pupils to sources of information for the purpose of . . .*

(**c**₁) *Acquiring or confirming facts or principles*

TEACHER 2   For homework I want you to read chapter . . . in your books and make notes of the properties of these gases.

T.O.S.—4

(c_2) *Identifying or solving problems*

TEACHER 1   Well, the thing to do now is to see if they move in and out, to try and move them in and out [referring to locust's mandibles].

(c_3) *Making inferences, formulating or testing hypotheses*

TEACHER 1   Right, we've got a short film showing some locusts feeding. I want you to look at it in your groups and then try to come up with some suggestions as to how the mouth parts cut the grass.

(c_4) *Seeking guidance on experimental procedure*

TEACHER 1   ... so you get rid of all the mouth parts [of the locust] at one time and when you have got them laid out you can then refer back to this sort of diagram. But you can see if you refer to this diagram where you are. You've removed this bit and you're now left with these two structures here, which if you look at the diagram are called mandibles, though they're not labelled on there but here are the mandibles ...

2d   Pupils seek information or consult for the purpose of ...

(d_1) *Acquiring or confirming facts or principles*

PUPIL 1   Is that its nose then [viewing a film loop on locusts feeding]?
PUPIL 2   Yes, I think so ...

(d_2) *Identifying or solving problems*

PUPIL 1   If you heat up some of the solution [potash alum] and then let it cool, we can see whether we get a precipitate. If we do, it must be saturated.
PUPIL 2   Yes.

(d_3) *Making inferences, formulating or testing hypotheses*

[Pupils watching film of locust feeding.]
PUPIL 1   I think they are moving.
PUPIL 2   It must be tasting it all the time.
PUPIL 3   Yes, I suppose so.
PUPIL 2   It looks as if they're always touching it.
PUPIL 1   They must be attached to the triangular things.
PUPIL 3   Yes.

2e   Pupils refer to teacher for the purpose of ...

(e_1) *Acquiring or confirming facts or principles*

PUPIL   Is this lime water cloudy, sir?
TEACHER 2   What do you think?
PUPIL   We think it is.

(e_2) *Seeking guidance when identifying or solving problems*

PUPIL   We've tried lime water and it's gone cloudy so it can't be oxygen, sir
TEACHER 2   Good, well done ...

(e₃) *Seeking guidance when making inferences, formulating or testing hypotheses*

PUPIL Well, we think it's either carbon dioxide or oxygen so we're going to try litmus. We don't know if it will dissolve.

TEACHER 2 Well, you'll have to take my word for it . . .

FURTHER EXAMPLES INVOLVING MORE COMPLEX INTERACTIONS

By way of further illustration, the following transcript involving Teacher 4 is given and analysed in order to show the association of several categories within a given sequence. Not all statements contained in this transcript will be examined, but merely some which pose more difficult problems. The extract is taken from the film *Exploring Chemistry*, available from Unilever Film Library. The teacher talks first to small groups about what they are doing—heating copper in a flame—and later to the whole class. For convenience, pupils are referred to as A, B, etc. in the dialogue.

[1] TEACHER 4 Right, now . . . what do you think?
     PUPIL 1 It went . . .
     PUPIL 2 It's turned silver, sir.
     TEACHER 4 Turned silver? Would you say it's silver? Take it out of the flame for a moment, have a look at it. What do you mean by silver?
[5] PUPIL 1 It seems to have gone . . . red.
     PUPILS   . . . green . . . orange . . .
     TEACHER 4 Yes, there's obviously a lot of changes going. What happens if you scrape that? . . .
     PUPIL 2 It's going . . . it . . .
     PUPIL 1 It goes pink . . .
[10] TEACHER 4 Do you think that's something that's formed on the outside, or what? What's happened to it?
     PUPIL 1 I think it's something formed to . . . to prevent the . . . copper inside from burning.
[12] TEACHER 4 What do you think is happening, then?
     PUPIL 1 A film's forming.
     TEACHER 4 A film . . .
[15] PUPIL 2 It's giving something out.
     TEACHER 4 It's giving something out. You think this is coming from inside the copper, do you?
     PUPIL 1 Yes.
     PUPIL 2 . . . combining with something in the air . . . to form the film.
     TEACHER 4 So you think something in the copper . . . is doing what?
[20] PUPIL 2 Is coming out . . . well, is combining with the air to form a black film.
     TEACHER 4 Yes. And what do *you* think?
     PUPIL 3 The same.
     TEACHER 4 You think the same? Well, *what* do you think—you tell me then . . . since you say you think the same.

PUPIL 3   I think . . . there is something coming out and combining with the air . . .

[25]   TEACHER 4   Something combining with the air? Do you think you could think up an experiment to see whether the air *is* important in this or not?

PUPIL 1   Yes . . . well . . . we could . . .

TEACHER 4   Well, I don't want to hear it yet. I'm going to ask you all in a moment when you are lined up round the bench. All right?

PUPIL 1   Right.

TEACHER 4   OK.

. . . .

[30]   TEACHER 4   Well where do you think it's coming from, this black colour?

PUPIL 3   The heat.

TEACHER 4   From . . . the flame?

[33]   PUPIL 3   Yes, sir.

TEACHER 4   You think it's something coming out of the flame?

[35]   PUPIL 3   Yes, sir.

TEACHER 4   See whether you can think up . . . You think it's coming out of the flame . . . [turning to another boy] Do you think it's coming out of the flame?

PUPIL 4   I think it's coming out of the copper, sir . . . something in the copper.

TEACHER 4   You think it's coming out of the copper? Well look, see whether you can think of things you could do, another experiment which would show which of you is correct. Anyway, look, think about it.

. . . .

[To the class gathered around the bench]

TEACHER 4   Right then. We've got three theories as to why the copper turns black when it's heated. We've got A's theory, which has six supporters, saying that it's something coming out of the air. We've got C's theory with four supporters saying that it's something coming out ot the flame. We've got F's theory with eighteen supporters saying it's something coming out of the copper. Now obviously you can't all be right—and you've had some time to think over and work out an experiment to help verify your theory. OK then, A . . . what's your experiment?

[40]   PUPIL 1   Well . . . suppose that's . . . air, I guess . . . it would be a good idea . . . um . . . to . . . um . . . put . . . a piece of copper foil in a . . . in a . . . in a tube and . . . and put a cork in the end, and then take the air out of it with a vacuum pump. And then heat it. If it turned black again, it would prove our idea was wrong, but if . . . if . . . if it doesn't change, our . . . it would be all right.

TEACHER 4   Do you agree with that, B?

PUPIL 2   Yes.

TEACHER 4   Good. Now, what do the flame people think? [No answer] What do you think, C?

PUPIL 3 Use another sort of foil and if that turned black then you'd know it was something in the flame. If it didn't, it wouldn't be something in the flame.

[45] TEACHER 4 Yes . . . any idea what particular foil?

[46] PUPIL 3 Lead foil? . . .

TEACHER 4 . . . All right, well, we'll try it . . . But can anyone think of a way by which they could heat the copper so that the flame won't actually come in contact with it? What could you do to . . . E, any ideas from this group?

PUPIL 4 Sir, you could . . . er . . . put copper foil in a test-tube over the flame. Then the flame won't be getting at the copper.

TEACHER 4 Good—that's a good idea, isn't it? If you heat—if you heat the copper in something where the flame's not actually touching . . . Now, F, you're the spokesman for the copper school. Now, have you got any ideas on this?

[50] PUPIL 5 Well, you . . . you could repeat . . . um . . . A's experiment, and if . . . um . . . if the copper turned black, that would prove us right . . . um . . . but if it turned . . . if it stayed its norm . . . it would prove A's group wrong as well.

Utterance 4: The first characteristic of this utterance is that it was made by the teacher in a sequence of utterances which were initiated by him. The second is that it contains both questions and direction. The questions 'Turned silver?' and 'Would you say it's silver?' appear to do no more than ask the pupil to confirm a previous observation, that is to say the questions and the directive which follows ('Take it out of the flame for a moment, have a look at it') seem to constitute a directive to the pupil to confirm a matter of fact. Therefore this utterance would be classified as c_1, *teacher directs pupils to sources of information for the purpose of acquiring or confirming facts and principles.*

Utterances 10 to 17: In this sequence the teacher again initiates the exchange. It is clear that 'Do you think that's something that's formed on the outside, or what?' and 'What do you think is happening, then?' constitute part of the same exchange and that the net function of these questions is to invite pupils to speculate. In utterance 10 the teacher calls for a variety of suggestions and in utterance 11 he gets one. Utterance 12 is therefore designed to prod the pupil into some kind of more detailed explanation. In 16 the teacher does not simply confirm that he agrees with the pupil's suggestion that a film is being formed. He takes it up and builds upon it in order to develop a hypothesis. Utterances 10, 12 and 16 are therefore all part of the same unit and should be classified under a_3, *teacher asks questions (or invites comments) which are answered by making hypothesis or speculation.* In this case there may remain some doubt as to whether the question asked by the teacher evoked in the pupil one or both of the behaviours, observing and speculating. The following procedure is recommended.

(i) Consider the interaction in context rather than attempting to classify each individual statement. Take note of the pupil's response.
(ii) If it is still impossible to distinguish a predominant category and there are grounds for believing that both behaviours are involved, then invoke Rule 3 and record both.

Utterances 25 to 28: Although, as written, utterance 25 constitutes a series of questions, they are in fact questions which do not call for an immediate answer regarding the design of an experiment. Functionally, these questions are directions in which the pupil is being asked to refer to objects and phenomena in order to test the hypothesis which the earlier discussion has brought to light. If an immediate reply had been obtained, a_4 would have been used. In response to the second question asked by the teacher, it may reasonably be inferred that the teacher would not accept a simple 'yes' or 'no' as adequate. It may also be inferred that the teacher expected the pupils to design an experiment to test their hypotheses but not to do this spontaneously as an immediate answer to the question put to them. The function of the question was to direct pupils to engage in an activity which we might describe as experimental design with the object of testing their hypotheses. The sequence is classified under c_3, *teacher directs pupils to sources of information for the purpose of making inferences, formulating or testing hypotheses.*

Utterance 39: Here the teacher recapitulates the hypotheses which had arisen during the previous pupil discussion. Under Rule 9 this is recorded as b_1.

Utterances 43 and 49: Here the teacher is asking the pupils to suggest ways in which the apparatus available can be manipulated in order to meet the requirements of the experiment. Therefore this utterance by the teacher would be classified under a_4, *teacher asks questions (or invites comments) which are answered by designing of experimental procedure.*

NOTE TO RULE 8

Subsequent use of the schedule has provided evidence that the distinctions made in Rule 8 require still further clarification. In particular, it is sometimes difficult to distinguish between recalling facts or observations previously made when an observer was not present. It is therefore suggested that all questions which do *not* relate to information obtained from pupil observation of objects or phenomena (including such records as photographs) *made during the course of the lesson* are excluded from categories a_5 and a_6. To sharpen the distinction between a_5 and a_6, Rule 8 should be modified to read:

When the pupil answers a question or makes a comment based upon observation *limited to factual statements,* and where neither the teacher demands nor the pupil gives any further elaboration, category a_5 is used. In all other cases, the question is recorded under a_6.

since when teachers were controlling the design of the experiment they would ask a_4 questions, but these would be accompanied by questions of a_1 and a_2 types. If the design of the experiment was determined wholly by answers from the pupils, then questions in the a_4 category would occur without accompanying a_1 and a_2 questions.

However, although this rationale was acceptable to the observers for the use of the schedule in the current project, it was felt that the schedule could be modified for future use. A possible alternative is to modify category a_1 and make it *recall of facts, principles and experimental procedures,* but this would blunt the instrument. Science teaching based on an inquiry approach necessarily involves designing experiments. In order to distinguish between teachers who do and teachers who do not involve pupils in designing experimental procedures, it would be desirable to keep category a_4 to be used exclusively for questions answered by pupils exercising a high level of skill in designing experiments. Additionally, it might be useful to add to the categories of questions, those which are *answered by the recall of experimental procedures.*

1b *Teacher makes statements . . .*
Only two minor difficulties were reported by the observers in this major category; these were in the minor category b_4, *teacher makes statements of experimental procedure.*

The first was the problem of classifying teacher statements concerning the treatment of experimental results. It was agreed by the observers to treat such statements as statements of experimental procedure. The second difficulty was in determining the line to be drawn between general procedural statements (which are not recorded in this schedule) and statements of *experimental* procedure. When the former are managerial in character, difficulties might arise. Instructions such as 'leave a one inch margin', 'apply a little water before inserting the glass tube into the rubber connexion', 'place the reagent bottle towards the centre of the bench when you have finished with it' are regarded as procedural statements of a more general kind, which are not recorded. It does not appear to be too difficult to identify those procedural statements which contain some instruction directly relevant to an experiment under discussion. Such statements might be 'place the leaf in boiling water in order to kill it', 'add about 10 cubic centimetres of 2N hydrochloric acid', 'connect the resistor in parallel with the light bulb'.

1c *Teacher directs pupils to sources of information for the purpose of . . .*
The original instructions on the use of directives took the form of the single paragraph on pp. 22–3 beginning 'Sources of information . . .' and concerning the use of Rule 10. As a result of the problems described below, the three further paragraphs beginning 'In all cases, behaviours are classified . . .' were included in the revised instructions on directives.

After analysis of the observers' performance in the test based on the first

3 Observers' reactions

The present form and contents of this observation schedule are the result of eighteen months of trials. The schedule has evolved by adaptation to the operational demands made on it. Because the parent research project on the Evaluation of Science Teaching Methods was of limited duration, it was necessary to call a halt to this evolutionary process. In order to produce an instrument in time to allow observations to take place during the second year of this three-year project, we had to be satisfied with the product of one year's developmental work on the schedule. This truncation of the developmental period was not as arbitrary as it may appear. Earlier versions of the schedule underwent relatively major changes; later versions were subject to diminishingly smaller modifications. The trend in this evolution has been towards simplification and facility of use.

It is unnecessary to outline all the steps in the evolutionary progress of the schedule, but it will be helpful to place on record the experience of the team of observers and their reactions to using it. The information fed back to us by the observers was invaluable in determining the published version of the *manual*, as well as giving clear indications of possible deficiencies in the schedule. The purpose of reporting general reactions and verbatim comments made by observers in letters, during training sessions, or in a major de-briefing session attended by more than half the observers, is to indicate to future users how the schedule might profitably be adapted or improved.

SOME PROBLEMS ASSOCIATED WITH PARTICULAR CATEGORIES

The categories which appear in the final version of the schedule as b_4, *teacher makes statements of experimental procedure*, and c_4, *teacher directs pupils to sources of information for the purpose of seeking guidance on experimental procedure*, had been omitted from the last pre-pilot version of the schedule. This decision was supported by evidence that when practical work occurred, other categories such as a_5 and a_6 were used; therefore in order to differentiate between teachers who engaged their classes in practical work and those who did not, b_4 and c_4 were at least partly redundant. Secondly, when classes were engaged in practical work, all teachers used categories b_4 and c_4 to a substantial degree. These categories therefore failed to differentiate between different styles of practical work. The observers, however, were, less than happy in situations where statements and directives were being given about experimental procedures which they were instructed not to record. The observers strongly supported the view that these categories should be replaced in the schedule. Accordingly categories b_4 and c_4 were restored. This situation was exactly paralleled by the fate of categories d_4 and e_4.

1a   *Teacher asks questions (or invites comments) which are answered by . . .*
Of the seven minor categories in this major category it was a_4, *designing of experimental procedure*, which observers found to be inappropriate for the behaviours observed. One observer commented:

'I am a bit bothered by questions on experimental design. They are often either recall or posed as a problem with one correct answer. The episode is a_4, but hardly the same as asking a student to design an experiment from scratch.'

Another observer's comment exemplifies this situation:

'A teacher might ask, "What control should we use?" but get no answer. He then says, "What aspect of photosynthesis have we investigated?" (Answer—the need for CO_2.) "What should we include in the belljar then?" (Answer—some CO_2.) "What is a good source of CO_2?" (Answer—bicarbonate.) The episode is clearly concerned with experimental design, but the design remains in the head of the teacher, it is not supplied by students who merely produce recall or "problem" answers to specific intermediate questions. To classify this as a question which is answered by designing of experimental procedures seems to defeat the purpose of the schedule. On the other hand, if the students go through this ritual often enough, it might be expected that they will eventually be good at designing at least a certain number or type of experiments. I tend to record this in a_4 *and* a_1/a_2.'

The original decision to include this category was based on the possibility that an open invitation to pupils to design an experiment to test some hypothesis, which had arisen out of a group's investigation, would differentiate teaching styles. Two types of problem affected the reliability of this category. First, the common usage of the word 'experiment' has resulted in a devaluation of the word to stand for almost any practical involvement. Secondly, an experimental design which fits the new situation may be the result of little more than *recall*. Furthermore, the participation by the teacher may vary from almost nil, where the pupils are left alone to design an appropriate experiment, to the other extreme where, by close questioning, the teacher leads the pupils to a design which is more a product of the teacher's thinking than the pupils'. A discussion of these issues at the de-briefing session was summarized thus:

It was felt that using category a_4 to record questions answered by experimental design would still provide information to distinguish between styles of teaching, reliability tape (see p. 11), which was used at the initial training sessions, it was found that there was some difficulty with the use of Rule 10 when applying it to situations in which the teacher is demonstrating before the class. The observers coded a section of the first reliability tape—a teacher carrying out a demonstration concerning the movement of bromine vapour up a tube, first with air present and then with the tube evacuated. The class were considering the problem of how to use measurement to get some idea of the means square velocity of the particles. During this episode the teacher talked continuously but, as far as one could observe from the television pictures, the pupils only listened and answered questions. The team classified these episodes as teacher talk under **1a** and **1b** but nearly half the observers placed it as a directive in c_2, *teacher directs pupils to sources of information* (i.e. apparatus) *for the purpose of identifying or solving problems.*

The essential point to note is that pupils in the filmed episode did not engage in activity independently of the teacher. They listened to teacher statements, answered teacher questions, but they neither produced a record of the experiment nor discussed questions raised by the teacher. Had they done so, such activity would have been classified in categories c_1 to c_3. A situation which exemplifies this might be the preparation of a gas in a chemistry lesson, where the pupils draw diagrams of the apparatus and make notes while the exercise is proceeding. Situations where the teacher dominates the action during the demonstration, and allows note-taking, apparatus drawing and discussion only *after* he has had his say, will be recorded initially either as a_1 to a_7 (questions) or as b_1 to b_4 (statements), and later as c_1 to c_4 (directives).

A further difficulty with the directives category may be illustrated by the following comments, reported verbatim from an observer's letter, and a part of a discussion of this problem which took place at the de-briefing session.

'I was uneasy about the situation where the teacher refers the class to a diagram on the board in the course of an account and asks a "problem" question. For example, "by looking at the shape of the stomach in this diagram can we see what one of its uses is?" If this were a statement, the "directive" to look at the diagram would be ignored. Is it ignored in the context of a question? (Answer was expected to be "storage".)'

In the discussion at the de-briefing session the following comments were made.

OBSERVER 1 c_2 or is it not? [Several yes's] It is information to solve a problem which the teacher has posed.

TEAM MEMBER 1   Is that generally agreed? The agreement seems to be that there is a directive here. I would have classified this as a question and have probably ignored the directive.

OBSERVER 2   I would have put it down as both. First of all he refers the kids to the board—'now look at the board'—and *then* he asks the question—*two* things.

OBSERVER 3   I think this is helping to pick out a certain kind of teacher, a teacher who uses a particular kind of visual aid as a source of question-asking.

TEAM MEMBER 1   I thought we had previously agreed that where the board was being used to back statements, we would ignore the directive to attend to whatever was illustrated on the board. The revised rule that we invented to assist you involved the instruction to *look at the kids and see what they are doing* during the process. Are they busy copying down what's on the board or are they listening to the teacher? Now when you extend this rule to the area of questioning, the same rule applies. If the information on the board is being used as a vehicle for questions, then we stick to the questioning category and we do not use the directive. The kind of distinction which I think the directive requires is to see if the question results in sustained activity.

TEAM MEMBER 2   There is also the question of the discreteness of events. The biologist with the stomach could have said without drawing a diagram, 'The stomach is sack shaped; what do you think its function is?' The teacher, as in this case, might draw a picture of a stomach and direct the pupils to look at the picture, and then ask them to speculate on its function. He might have shown them a photograph or he might have instructed them to dissect a mouse, observe the stomach and then speculate on its function. We need to isolate the discrete behaviour package and say at this point it was a directive. I think it must be an arbitrary rule, that unless the pupils engage in *sustained* activity after the directive then it was not a directive.

OBSERVER 2   There's a sort of active involvement in the sort of situation I came across, where the pupils developed a hypothesis about whether moles of elements will occupy the same volume or not. The teacher says, "Well, how are we going to find this out? We'd better look it up in our book of data." Then there is a big pause and the information goes up on the board. That really is teacher directs.

In order also to draw attention to the problem of using the schedule while the teacher was carrying out a demonstration, a number of other cases brought by observers were discussed. It was felt that there is a distinct difference between a teacher giving information while using an experimental demonstration as an aid and a teacher simply standing before the pupils and telling them the information. If a directive from the teacher is identified because it results in some sustained activity of the pupils, it would be very difficult to include teacher demonstration in this category since it would involve difficult judgements by the observer. The type of judgement made would relate to whether or not the pupils were actively engaging in thinking about what they could see. If the latter approach is rejected, the only alternative left is that teacher utterances accompanying a demonstration are usually recorded as questions or statements. Some observers felt that this would lower the status of a demonstration, making it equivalent to statements or questions not accompanied by apparatus. Suggestions of how to overcome this problem included the possible introduction of a new category, say b_5, *teacher makes statements reinforced by demonstration*, or even *teacher demonstrates*. Another idea was to introduce a new major category of *teacher demonstrates* ..., containing subordinate categories to acquire facts, solve problems, test hypotheses, so that when a teacher is doing a demonstration, the observer can record what sort of demonstration he is doing and why he is doing it.

At present the difficulties remain partly unsolved, although the consensus among observers was to continue to operate the directive categories with the revised rules now given in the manual.

GENERAL COMMENTS

Validity

The Science Teaching Observation Schedule was designed to record intellectual transactions occurring in science lessons, particularly those transactions which facilitated a differentiation between contrasted teaching styles. Some observers, all of whom had several years' experience of observing students in training, found the instruction to record only intellectual transactions disconcerting. While most observers were satisfied that the schedule enabled valid distinctions to be made between teaching styles, two observers' critical comments should be noted.

OBSERVER 1   A system of ticks does no credit to this lesson: Mr X had established a rapport with his class which enabled the lesson to proceed very smoothly. He started by asking questions, was very friendly, often humorous; everyone was working and seemed to be concentrating all the time.

TEAM MEMBER   I am not quite sure what the criticism is here. 'A system of ticks does no credit to the lesson'; I am sure that it does not, the problem is whether it records such events which distinguish between this teacher's performance and that of another teacher. I should hope that a system of ticks would possibly never do justice to a lesson in one sense. The problem is not that of doing justice to a lesson but of determining, when you think back over a lesson, that the system of ticks provides a profile of the intellectual transactions which comes near to matching the intellectual transactions as they occur.

OBSERVER 2   Isn't that comment trying to mirror the fact that the way the teacher relates to the pupils, his sympathy and so on, just doesn't come through as it is not meant to do, the affective side isn't included.

TEAM MEMBER   Are, then, the deficiencies mainly due to the exclusion of affective behaviours? If you are right in believing that the affective relationships that a teacher establishes are a great deal more important in determining pupil gains—either affective or cognitive—than the intellectual transactions which we are recording, then we will fail to establish the relationships which we are looking for. However, if there is a shortfall between how you saw the intellectual activities in the class and the array of ticks on the schedule then this gives me cause for concern.

Another observer shared the view that information not recorded in the schedule might be more significant in determining pupil gains. His focus was mainly managerial but with affective overtones.

'Can I bring up a general point . . . I haven't really formulated it properly in my mind, but I think that this project is looking at teaching methods, and yet you are going to test what the pupils have learned. Two questions arise; why do I spend so much time training my students about management of classes? Presumably because we think this in some way affects the learning and this is not recorded at all. And another thing, I am also unhappy with the time sampling units. An event may be recorded as a tick when its duration was ten seconds. But we may not record what happens in the other 170 seconds. We go into a class and a person is talking and doing the same thing for one minute or for three minutes, and the record is the same. In another class a person may spend ten seconds saying something and spend the rest of the time telling the kids to shut up and sit down. The record will be the same but obviously one group is likely to learn more than the other.

In the face of these criticisms, it is necessary to reiterate the rationale behind the restriction of our attention to intellectual transactions. We are interested in possible correlations between teaching style defined in terms of intellectual transactions and pupil gains, both cognitive and affective. While it is true that affective transactions and managerial efficiency may limit these gains, we hope that such limitations only operate (so as seriously to affect gains) outside a normal range of variation. Our observers at the end of each lesson wrote their own account of the events which occurred. It is our hope that any breakdown due to affective or managerial failure would have been noted in these accounts. If there is any shortcoming here, it is in the research design and not in the schedule.

Observer effects
The problem of artefacts due to the presence of an observer or his equipment is of universal concern to those who have attempted to record events taking place in classrooms as they occur. Some of our observers entertained doubts about the freedom from such effects of the events they observed, as the following quotes from their comments show.

OBSERVER 1   I find some conflict between my neutral observer position and that part of the administration instructions which suggest that we should not attend atypical lessons. My sample of teachers occasionally gingered up their lessons with demonstrations, but the amount of pupil–pupil and pupil–teacher interaction is generally low and the implied question, 'I hope that suited you', which follows a virtuoso chalk-and-talk performance promotes frustration when the effort is made to maintain the 'undisturbed by observer' position. Clearly the total sample will reveal complete coverage of the schedule and teaching styles and I would welcome some hint of the location of my observations within the complete range. Generally my sample of teachers appear pretty bewildered by the experiment and unsure of whether they are providing what we want. I can't tell them!

TEAM MEMBER   This raises the more general issue of how far do we think, by our presence, we influence the teacher's style. We hoped that if teachers did change their style it would be marginal and they'd go to a more extreme form of their own style. But these expectations are somewhat speculative, as you will realize.

OBSERVER 2   The pupils, perhaps more than the teachers, are influenced by our presence in the room.

OBSERVER 3   I think in the London area it would be abnormal if there were not a visitor in the room.

OBSERVER 4   What greatly surprised me was that my two teachers teach with an almost identical style. I thought at first this was an act put on for our benefit, but now I have seen six of these lessons and talked to the children and the teachers, and I am quite convinced this is just what they do. It is slightly exaggerated, yes, it is a little more perfect than it should be but the whole atmosphere is really very relaxed. I am sure it is just what they normally do.

Sampling problems

The use of any recording system including both electronic recording and human observers inevitably involves selection. No system can attend to all pupils, to all events, simultaneously. Even when the selection of events to be observed is limited, in this case to intellectual transactions, a further constraint is imposed by the physical conditions under which observation occurs—for example, the location of the observer, noise levels and the like. There is no doubt that when a teacher is engaged in a dialogue with a class, observers find events easier to record than when a class is involved in group work. One observer considered that when a teacher was talking with a small group of pupils, conditions were ideal for using the schedule, but as the group size increased there was a growing uncertainty of the record's accuracy.

OBSERVER 1   I can record intellectual transactions between the teacher and a small group of pupils and this is reflected in the schedule. If, however, we are sitting at the back of a class, we very often know that what has been recorded are the intellectual transactions between the front two benches. Something quite different happened with the rest.

OBSERVER 2   That merely reflects the fact that when a teacher is teaching, not all the kids are engaged on learning. Learning and teaching are inefficient things but when there is active engagement the schedule records the intellectual events adequately.

Group work, when simultaneously groups may engage in different activities, presents similar problems. Although this problem can be ameliorated when the observer positions himself strategically to pick up as much of the action as possible, there is no ideal solution to the problem. Some recording systems have built into them categories for estimates of the number or proportion of pupils involved in a given activity. A refinement of this type could be added to the schedule.

One observer who found himself observing a biology lesson involving practical work on the playing fields in which heart rates were measured over a 300 metre run commented, 'The intellectual transactions over a range of 300 metres are difficult to keep track of.'

General reactions of observers and teachers
The subjective reactions of observers and teachers are not presented here as conclusive evidence to establish the validity of the instrument, but many unsolicited favourable comments from observers have been encouraging. At an early stage in the research project, it had been suggested that teachers would not tolerate the presence of an observer. This prediction was proved entirely false; some teachers wrote to the project team and asked to participate in the research, knowing what it involved.The following comment by an observer is an optimistic note with which to conclude this account:

'On the positive side, teachers are welcoming and kind and the observations are made in the best circumstances. The schedule—for me at least—sharply differentiates between different teaching styles. The opportunity to look at experienced teachers at work is beyond price, my attitude to student teachers has been profoundly affected.'